ALL-TIME BEST
WNBA Players

BY ELLEN LABRECQUE

Lisa Leslie ▶

The Child's World
childsworld.com

Published by The Child's World®
1980 Lookout Drive • Mankato, MN 56003-1705
800-599-READ • www.childsworld.com

Photographs
Cover: Lucy Nicholson/AP Images.
AP Images: Cal Sports Media 5; Steve Yeater 10;
Elaine Thompson 13; Mark J. Terrill 14. Newscom:
George Bridges/KRT 2; Mingo Nesmith/Icon SW 6;
Tony Quinn/Icon SW 9; Jerry Holt/TNS 17; Javon
Moore/Cal Sport Media 18; Harry Walker/KRT 21.

ISBN 9781503835290
LCCN 2019944742
Printed in the United States of America

Contents

What Makes a Great Player?

What makes a great WNBA player? Is it the way she can score often? On defense, does she stick like glue to each **opponent**? Does she lead her team to win after win? How about *all* of the above? Meet the eight best players in WNBA history. Each player is an incredible scorer and a solid defender. They're all amazing winners! There is no match for this great eight.

Two superstars battle on the court. Maya Moore (left) has led her team to four WNBA championships. Candace Parker was a two-time WNBA MVP. ▶

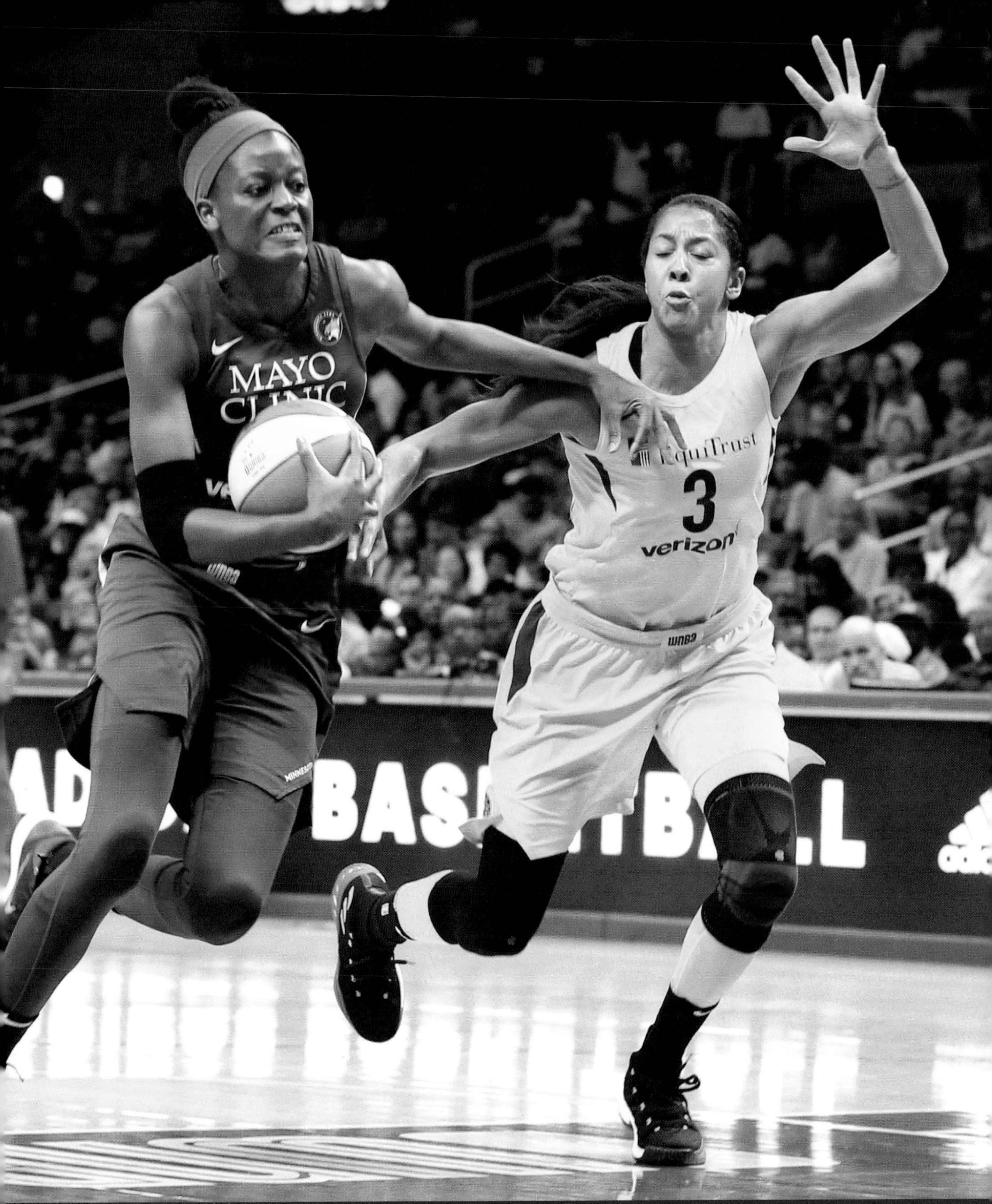
MAYO
3
verizon

Sue Bird

Sue Bird has played for the Seattle Storm since 2002. As a **point guard**, she runs the show. She makes one smooth pass after another. Bird makes no-look and behind-the-back **assists** look easy. She has dished more than 2,800 assists. That's a WNBA record! Bird also knows how to win. She led the Storm to WNBA titles in 2004, 2010, and 2018.

Team: Seattle
Height: 5'9" (1.75 m)
Position: Guard
College: Connecticut
Joined WNBA: 2002

Bird shows off perfect form for a chest pass to a teammate.

Tamika Catchings

Tamika Catchings played 15 great seasons with the Indiana Fever (2002–2016). Catchings led the Fever to the WNBA title in 2012. In the final game, she scored 25 points and was named the Finals **MVP**. Catchings was born with hearing loss in both ears. She didn't let that stop her. She learned to use her other senses more. "I became very **observant** on the court," she says. "Sometimes it feels like I can see things before they happen."

Team: Indiana
Height: 6'1" (1.85 m)
Position: Forward
College: Tennessee
Joined WNBA: 2002

Catchings was named to 10 WNBA All-Star games in her great career. ▶

Yolanda Griffith

Team: Sacramento
Height: 6'4" (1.94 m)
Position: Center
College: Fla. Atlantic
Joined WNBA: 1999

"**Y**o Yo" was a powerful force near the basket. She was super at blocking shots and grabbing **rebounds**. In 1999, her first season in the league, Griffith was named the league MVP. She was named the defensive player of the year. She played 11 seasons (1999–2009) for three different teams. In 2005, she led the Sacramento Monarchs to the WNBA championship. Points didn't mean much to her. "Doesn't matter how much I score," she said. "As long as we win."

Griffith was a strong, powerful player. Few players could guard her well.

Lauren Jackson

Lauren Jackson was the **center** of the Storm—the Seattle Storm, that is. This Australian was a scoring, shot-blocking machine. She also had a very cool style. She changed her hair color all the time. Jackson was named the league MVP three times (2003, 2007, 2010). She helped Seattle win the 2004 and 2010 championships. Three times she led the WNBA in scoring. "She's definitely the best," said longtime teammate Sue Bird.

Team: Seattle

Height: 6'6" (1.98 m)

Position: Forward

None (Australia)

Joined WNBA: 2001

Jackson scored 739 points in 2007. She was the WNBA MVP that season! ▶

Lisa Leslie

Team: Los Angeles

Height: 6'5" (1.96 m)

Position: Center

College: USC

Joined WNBA: 1997

Lisa Leslie helped put the WNBA on the sports map. She was the league's biggest star in 1997, its first season. She later was the first player to **dunk** in a WNBA game! Leslie played 12 super seasons for the Los Angeles Sparks. She also worked as a model and actress. On the court, Leslie led the Sparks to WNBA titles in 2001 and 2002. In 2015, she was elected to the Basketball Hall of Fame!

Leslie was the WNBA MVP in 2001, 2004, and 2006.

Maya Moore

Maya Moore is a winner! The **forward** joined the Minnesota Lynx in 2011. Through 2018, Moore led her team to four WNBA titles (2011, 2013, 2015, 2017). The Lynx finished second in the league in 2012 and 2016. Lynx coach Cheryl Reeve called Moore "the perfect superstar." Moore is an all-around player who can strike from the outside or drive to the basket. Plus, in eight seasons, she only missed one regular-season game.

Team: Minnesota
Height: 6'0" (1.83 m)
Position: Forward
College: Connecticut
Joined WNBA: 2011

Moore took the 2019 WNBA season off to work in her ministry. She plans to return in 2020.

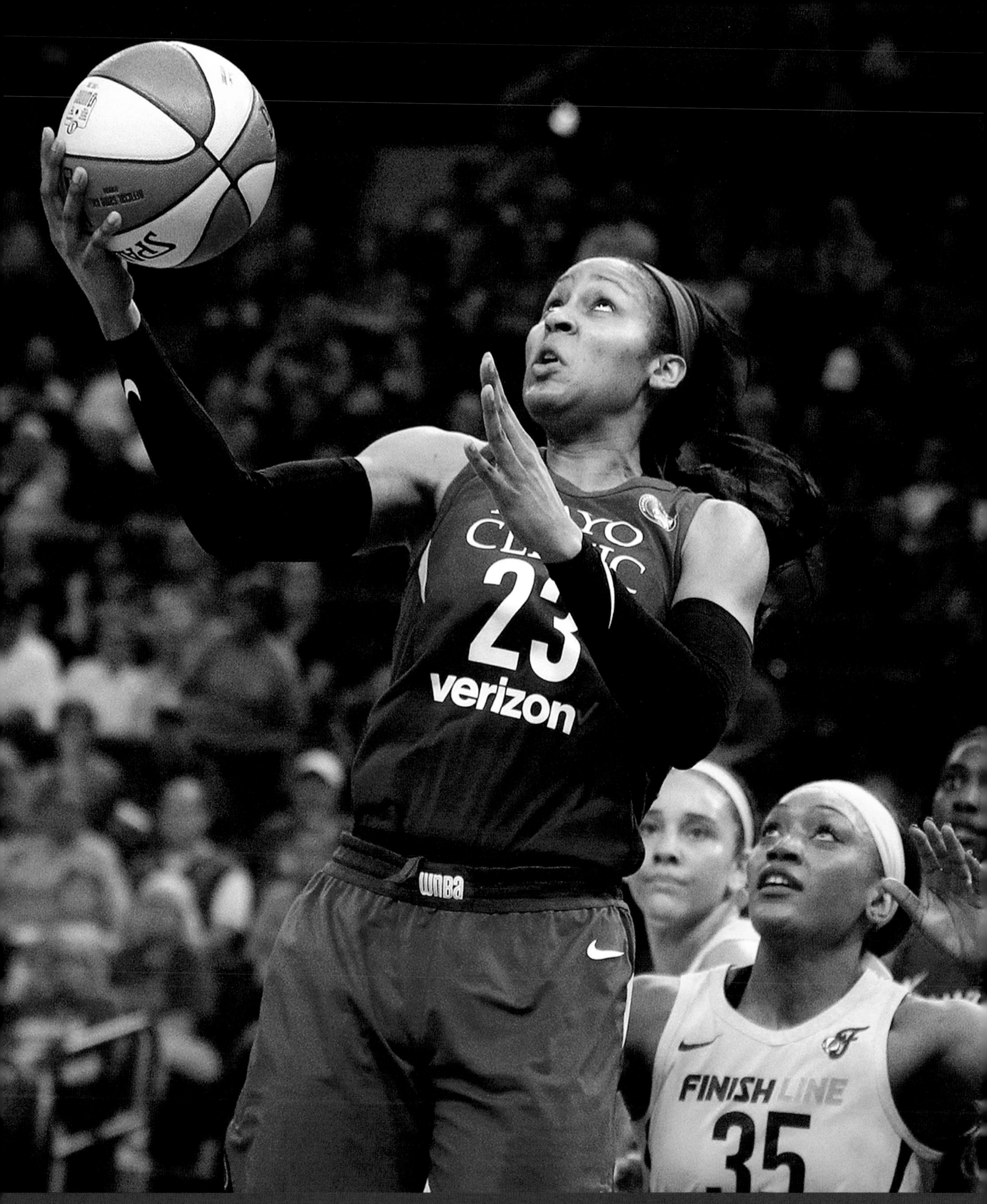
23
verizon
WNBA
FINISH LINE
35

Candace Parker

In 2008, Candace Parker became the first WNBA player to be the MVP and Rookie of the Year in the same season. The high-scoring forward was the second WNBA player to dunk. She won the MVP again in 2013 and led the Sparks to a title in 2016. Parker has played her whole career for the Los Angeles Sparks. She has also worked as a TV announcer for basketball games.

Team: Los Angeles

Height: 6'4" (1.75 m)

Position: Forward

College: Tennessee

Joined WNBA: 2008

◀ Parker has also played in Russia, Turkey, and China.

Sheryl Swoopes

Sheryl Swoopes had a game as smooth as her name. She made playing like an All-Star look easy. Swoopes was the first player signed to the WNBA in 1997. She led the Houston Comets to four straight WNBA titles. During their first title run, she had just come back from having a baby! She played 12 WNBA seasons. She was the MVP in 2000, 2002, and 2005. In 2016, she was elected to the Basketball Hall of Fame.

Team: Houston

Height: 6'0" (1.83 m)

Position: Forward

College: Texas Tech

Joined WNBA: 1997

Sheryl was the first female player to have a basketball shoe named for her. They were called "Air Swoopes."

Glossary

assist (uh-SIST) a pass that leads directly to a basket

center (SEN-ter) the basketball position that plays closest to the basket

dunk (DUNK) a shot in which a player slams or stuffs the ball into the basket

forward (FORE-wurd) the basketball position that scores and rebounds

MVP most valuable player

observant (ub-ZERV-ent) able to pay close attention to what one sees

opponent (uh-POH-nunt) the team that is on the opposite side of your team

point guard (POYNT GARD) the basketball position that directs the team by making passes

rebound (REE-bownd) to grab the ball after a missed shot

Find Out More

IN THE LIBRARY

Delle Donne, Elena. *Full-Court Press*. New York, NY:
Harper Entertainment, 2018.
(Note: This is a novel by the Washington Mystics' star player.)

Littlejohn, James and Matt Shipley. *B is for Baller: The Ultimate
Basketball Alphabet*. Chicago, IL: Triumph Books, 2018.

Schaller, Bob and Dave Harnish. *The Everything Kids'
Basketball Book*. Avon, MA: Avon Media, 2017.

ON THE WEB

Visit our Web site for links about the
WNBA All-time Great Players:
childsworld.com/links

Note to Parents, Teachers, and Librarians:
We routinely verify our Web links to make sure they are safe
and active sites. So encourage your readers to check them out!

Index

About the Author

Ellen Labrecque has written more than 100 books for children. A former editor at *Sports Illustrated Kids* Magazine, she loves covering and watching the WNBA. She played basketball in college, where she was named to the Academic All-America team. She lives in Bucks County, Pennsylvania, with her husband and two kids.